NO-NONSENSE KEY

Read *The New Tax Law and What It Means to You*

- If you want an easy-to-read, understandable explanation of the Tax Reform Act of 1986

- If you want quickly to understand how the new law affects you

- If you want to know your IRA potential under the new law

- If you want to know how the new law affects your investments

NO-NONSENSE FINANCIAL GUIDES:

How to Finance Your Child's College Education
How to Use Credit and Credit Cards
Understanding Treasury Bills and Other U.S. Government Securities
Understanding Tax-Exempt Bonds
Understanding Money Market Funds
Understanding Mutual Funds
Understanding IRAs
Understanding Common Stocks
Understanding the Stock Market
Understanding Stock Options and Futures Markets
How to Choose a Discount Stockbroker
How to Make Personal Financial Planning Work for You
How to Plan and Invest for Your Retirement
Understanding Estate Planning and Wills
The New Tax Law and What It Means to You

NO-NONSENSE REAL ESTATE GUIDES:

Understanding Condominiums and Co-ops
Understanding Buying and Selling a House
Understanding Mortgages
Refinancing Your Mortgage

NO-NONSENSE FINANCIAL GUIDE

THE NEW TAX LAW AND WHAT IT MEANS TO YOU

Your Guide to the Tax Reform Act of 1986

Phyllis C. Kaufman
& Arnold Corrigan

LONGMEADOW PRESS

This publication describes the Tax Reform Act of 1986, which became law in October 1986. The information concerning the Act may change as a result of rules and regulations promulgated by or interpretations of the Internal Revenue Service, judicial interpretation or decisions, or technical corrections, additions, or amendments to the Act.

This publication is designed to provide accurate and authoritative information with regard to the subject matter covered. It is sold with the understanding that neither the publisher nor the authors are engaged in rendering legal, accounting, or other professional service regarding the subject matter covered. This publication is not to be used as a substitute for legal, accounting, or other professional advice.

The New Tax Law and What It Means to You

Cover art copyright © 1986 by Longmeadow Press.
Design by Adrian Taylor
Production services by William S. Konecky Associates, New York.

Published for Longmeadow Press, 201 High Ridge Road, Stamford, Connecticut 06904.

ISBN: 0-681-40184-2

Printed in the United States of America

9 8 7 6 5 4 3 2

To Carolyn Engel Temin and Martin Heller,
whose friendship makes life many shades brighter

ACKNOWLEDGEMENTS

The authors are especially grateful to Jules I. Whitman, Esquire, of the Philadelphia law firm of Dilworth, Paxson, Kalish and Kauffman, for sharing his deep knowledge and insight in the preparation of this book. We are also grateful to John W. Schmehl, Esquire, William E. Kirwan, Esquire, and other members of that firm.

We also wish to thank Peter Hart and John B. Stine, II, of Price Waterhouse, Philadelphia, for their kind cooperation; and we thank Sanford L. Fox for his thoughtful suggestions.

TABLE OF CONTENTS

Part V—Miscellaneous Provisions

Tables—How the Tax Rates Change, 1986–1988

INTRODUCTION

How will the Tax Reform Act of 1986 affect you? That depends on your income bracket, the size of your family, and what deductions you took in the past.

Some people will pay less tax, some more. While as many as 6 million low-income taxpayers will be eliminated from the tax rolls, the House-Senate Conference Report estimated that approximately 40% of taxpayers with income between $50,000 and $75,000 and 55% of taxpayers with income between $75,000 and $100,000 will pay more under the reform legislation.

In broadest terms, the new law taxes individuals at lower rates and in just a few simple brackets. But many of the deductions that used to be taken in figuring taxable income have now been partially or wholly eliminated. As a result, the benefits (or disadvantages) will vary widely.

Taxpayers who previously had only small deductions are likely to find that they are better off because of the lower rates and the higher standard deduction. Large families will benefit from a sizable increase in the personal exemption.

On the other hand, many middle- and upper-income taxpayers will find that they no longer can take deductions for contributions to their IRAs. And the big tax break on long-term capital gains has been eliminated.

Taxpayers who previously took large itemized deductions or who entered into tax shelter arrangements may find the new bill painful. But taxpayers who make $150,000 or $200,000 or more, and who have not cut their taxes sharply in the past through tax shelter arrangements, may find their tax bills substantially reduced.

How will it all affect you? This book will try to give you some important answers. But remember that the new tax Act is complicated and that it will be followed by equally complicated rules and regulations. We urge you to consult your tax professional for advice on how tax reform affects your specific situation.

1

A *NO-NONSENSE* SUMMARY OF THE TAX REFORM ACT

The new tax law can be confusing. For your convenience, we begin with the following reference table showing various provisions, a synopsis of the old law and new changes, and the effective date of each change. For details on each area, consult the chapters that follow.

Comparison of New Tax Law with Old Tax Law

ITEM	OLD TAX LAW	NEW TAX LAW	EFFECTIVE DATE
Individual Tax Rates	15 tax brackets, from 11% to 50%	2 tax brackets, 15% and 28%, with a 5% surtax (total 33%) on higher incomes within specified range	1/1/88 (partial in 1987)
Personal Exemption	$1,080	$2,000 ($1,900 in 1987, $1,950 in 1988)	1/1/89
Standard Deduction	$2,480 (Single) 3,670 (married filing jointly) 1,835 (married filing separately) 2,480 (head of household)	$3,000 (single) 5,000 (married filing jointly) 2,500 (married filing separately) 4,400 (head of household)	1/1/88

Comparison of New Tax Law with Old Tax Law

ITEM	OLD TAX LAW	NEW TAX LAW	EFFECTIVE DATE
Mortgage Interest	100% deductible	deductible for two residences up to amount of basis plus improvements (and loans for education and medical expenses)	1/1/87
Consumer Interest	100% deductible	deduction eliminated	1/1/87 (5-year phase-out)
State & Local Taxes	100% deductible	income and property taxes 100% deductible; sales tax not deductible	1/1/87
Medical Expenses	deductible over 5% of adjusted gross income	deductible over 7.5% of adjusted gross income	1/1/87
Charitable Contributions	deductible for all taxpayers	deductible only if taxpayer itemizes	1/1/87
Unreimbursed Employee Business Expenses	fully deductible	deductible above 2% of AGI floor as itemized deductions	1/1/87
Marriage Penalty (Two-Earner Deduction)	up to $3,000 deductible	deduction eliminated	1/1/87
Earned Income Credit	tax credit up to $550, income limit $11,000	maximum credit $800, income limit raised	1/1/87
Social Security	partially taxed above certain income levels	no change	1/1/87
Unemployment Compensation	partially taxed	fully taxed	1/1/87

Comparison of New Tax Law
with Old Tax Law

ITEM	OLD TAX LAW	NEW TAX LAW	EFFECTIVE DATE
Income Averaging	allowed	not allowed	1/1/87
Dividend Exclusion	$200 exclusion for couples; $100 for single taxpayer	exclusion repealed	1/1/87
Capital Gains	60% of long-term gains excluded from tax (20% maximum effective rate)	fully taxed (28% maximum in 1987 only)	1/1/87
IRA	up to $2,000 deductible	deduction subject to income limits if covered by company plan	1/1/87
401(k)	maximum $30,000 deduction	total limit unchanged but elective portion limited to $7,000	1/1/87
Adjustment for Inflation	applies to tax brackets, personal exemption, and standard deduction	no change	1/1/87
Alternative Minimum Tax	20% rate	21% rate, with greater applicability	1/1/87
Unearned Income of Minor (under age 14)	taxed at child's tax rate	taxed at top parental tax rate	1/1/87
Clifford Trusts	permitted	not permitted	3/1/86
Spousal Remainder Trusts	permitted	not permitted	3/1/86
Business Meal Expenses	100% deductible	80% deductible	1/1/87

Comparison of New Tax Law with Old Tax Law

ITEM	OLD TAX LAW	NEW TAX LAW	EFFECTIVE DATE
Business Entertainment Expenses	100% deductible	80% deductible	1/1/87
Corporate Tax Rates	graduated rates, 46% maximum (5% surtax between $1,000,000 and $1,405,000)	graduated rates, 34% maximum (5% surtax between $100,000 and $335,000)	7/1/87

PART 1
HOW IS INCOME TAXED?

2

WHAT IS INCOME?

The Tax Reform Act of 1986 makes relatively few changes in the rules as to what types of income are taxed. Some of the major types of income that must be reported on your federal income tax return are as follows:

- Wages, salaries, bonuses and commissions
- Fees and tips
- Certain fringe benefits
- Dividends
- Interest
- Social Security benefits (see below)
- Unemployment compensation
- Alimony
- Pensions and annuities
- Distributions from retirement plans
- Certain sick pay and disability pensions
- Capital gains
- Profits from a business or profession
- Rents and royalties
- Income from trusts
- Prizes and awards
- Illegal income

Some of the types of income *not* subject to federal income tax are as follows:

- Welfare benefits
- Veterans' benefits
- Workmen's compensation benefits
- Child support payments
- Gifts
- Inheritances

- Life insurance proceeds received on account of death
- Interest on certain state and local bonds
- Certain property insurance recoveries

Unemployment compensation paid to you under federal or state law was previously taxable to you only if your *total* income exceeded certain levels. Under the new law, unemployment compensation is fully taxable.

Social Security continues to be partly taxable for individuals with income above certain levels.

Scholarships and fellowships, which previously were excluded from income for tax purposes, will now be partially taxable. See Chapter 23.

But while the list of items that make up your "gross income" for IRS purposes may not change much, certain special parts of the list have acquired new significance. Items classified as *investment income* must be tracked with extra care, because the interest you pay on investment-related borrowings will only be deductible to the extent that it does not exceed "net investment income." See Chapter 16.

Also, in a massive change that will eliminate most "tax shelter" losses, the new law distinguishes *passive activity income*—income from a business or activity in which the taxpayer does not personally participate in a material way. Broadly speaking, expenses in these "passive" activities will now only be deductible from income in the same type of activity. This means that losses from tax shelters can no longer be used to reduce the tax on other types of income. See Chapter 18.

Capital Gains—The preferential treatment of long-term capital gains has been eliminated under the new Act. Capital gains will be taxed as ordinary income beginning in 1988. In 1987, capital gains will be taxed at ordinary income rates, but with a maximum of 28%. See Chapter 16.

Dividends you receive on stock are fully taxable as income. The exclusion of $100 for a single taxpayer and $200 for married taxpayers has been repealed.

3

TWO TAX BRACKETS OR THREE?

The Tax Reform Act of 1986 dramatically reduces the number of tax brackets and the maximum tax rates. The number of tax brackets is cut, according to the law's sponsors, from 15 to 2—though, as we shall see, there is really a third bracket tucked into the schedule. The maximum individual tax rate is lowered from 50% to 28%. Here's how the basic rates will look in 1988:

Taxable Income			1988 Tax Rate
Married Filing Jointly*	Single	Head of Household**	
$0 – 29,750	$0 – 17,850	$0 – 23,900	**15%**
Over 29,750	Over 17,850	Over 23,900	**28%**

The new system will not go into full effect until 1988. In 1987, a "blended system," combining the old rates and the new rates, will be in effect. Here are the basic 1987 rates:

Taxable Income			1987 Tax Rate
Married Filing Jointly*	Single	Head of Household**	
$0 – 3,000	$0 – 1,800	$0 – 2,500	**11%**
3,000 – 28,000	1,800 – 16,800	2,500 – 23,000	**15%**
28,000 – 45,000	16,800 – 27,000	23,000 – 38,000	**28%**
45,000 – 90,000	27,000 – 54,000	38,000 – 80,000	**35%**
over 90,000	over 54,000	over 80,000	**38.5%**

* As under the old law, for the year in which a spouse dies, the surviving spouse may be treated as married filing jointly.

** You may be eligible to file as a head of household if you were unmarried on the last day of the year and if you have maintained a home for yourself and a child or a dependent relative, or if you maintain a home for your parent(s) under certain conditions.

Taxable Income

But wait! Before you compare your new tax rates with the old, three words of warning:

First, the phrase "taxable income" has a different definition under the new law than under the old. Under the old law, as we shall see in Chapter 5, taxable income is figured before deducting the standard deduction, or "zero bracket amount," the standard deduction being built into the tax tables. Under the new law, the standard deduction is subtracted to arrive at "taxable income."

Second, even if you understand the change in the definition of taxable income, you can't accurately estimate your new tax until you have reviewed the major changes the new law makes in exemptions and deductions.

Third, in the wonderful world of tax reform, two equals three, at least when it comes to tax brackets.

The Third Bracket

Yes, for all practical purposes, the 1988 schedule actually includes three brackets—15%, 28%, and 33%. The 33% bracket results from the imposition of a 5% *surtax* on top of the "maximum" rate of 28%.

Actually, there are two different 5% surtaxes. But since the second one begins at exactly the income bracket where the first one ends, we will often refer to them as one. The surtaxes apply over the range of income shown in the tables below. For upper-income taxpayers, the first surtax is intended to offset the advantage of the lower 15% tax rate on the first "slice" of taxable income. For persons with taxable income over $89,560 (single) or over $149,250 (married), the effect will be very much as though *all* income were taxed at a flat rate of 28%. The second surtax cuts in above those income levels to wipe out the benefits of the personal exemption. (See Chapter 4.)

The tables shown above gave you the two basic tax brackets for 1988 and beyond. But the *real* tax brackets, *including the two surtaxes*, will be as follows:

Married Couple Filing Jointly

Taxable Income	Tax Rate
$0 – $ 29,750	15%
29,750 – 71,900	28%
71,900 – 149,250	33% (5% surtax)
149,250 – 171,090*	33% (second 5% surtax)
over 171,090	28%

Single

Taxable Income	Tax Rate
$0 – $ 17,850	15%
17,850 – 43,150	28%
43,150 – 89,560	33% (5% surtax)
89,560 – 100,480*	33% (second 5% surtax)
over 100,480	28%

Married Filing Separately

Taxable Income	Tax Rate
$0 – $ 14,875	15%
14,875 – 35,950	28%
35,950 – 113,300	33% (5% surtax)
113,300 – 124,220*	33% (second 5% surtax)
over 124,220	28%

Head of Household

Taxable Income	Tax Rate
$0 – $ 23,900	15%
23,900 – 61,650	28%
61,650 – 123,790	33% (5% surtax)
123,790 – 134,710*	33% (second 5% surtax)
over 134,710	28%

All the above brackets are indexed for inflation, so that they will be adjusted annually in 1989 and beyond.

* The 33% bracket ("surtax bracket") assumes two personal exemptions for a married couple and one for a single person, married person filing separately, or head of household. *The bracket is extended upward by an additional $10,920 of income for each additional exemption, including children.* For those who care about the mathematics: each exemption in 1988 saves the taxpayer $546 of tax (28% × $1,950 = $546). A 5% tax on $10,920 of income offsets this (5% × $10,920 = $546).

PART II
DEDUCTIONS FROM TAXABLE INCOME

4

PERSONAL EXEMPTION

While the Tax Reform Bill of 1986 takes away or curtails many deductions that taxpayers previously enjoyed, it offers a big boost in the personal exemption and in the standard deduction. This helps everyone, and it takes millions of the lowest-income taxpayers off the tax rolls entirely—especially families with several children, since each child counts as an additional exemption.

Each taxpayer may claim an exemption for him/herself, spouse and each dependent. The new Act increases the personal exemption as follows:

Year	Amount of Personal Exemption
1986	$1,080
1987	1,900
1988	1,950
1989	2,000
1990 and after	2,000 plus an adjustment for inflation. The inflation adjustment will be calculated to the nearest lowest multiple of $50, rather than to the nearest $10, as in the old law.

Tax Return of a Dependent

A person who is claimed as a dependent on another's tax return will not be entitled to any personal exemption on his/her own tax return. However, such a person can take all or part of the standard deduction under special rules. See Chapter 5.

Elderly and Blind

The additional personal exemptions that were available to an elderly (age 65 or over) or blind individual under the old act have been eliminated by the new Act and replaced by an additional standard deduction. See Chapter 5.

5

STANDARD DEDUCTION

As we said previously, the new tax law sharply increases the amount of the standard deduction—the deduction that can be taken by everyone who does not claim large itemized deductions.

Zero Bracket Amount

And as we also noted, there is an important change in the method of calculation.

Under the previous law, the standard deduction was referred to as the "zero bracket amount"—that is, the amount of income not subject to any tax. This amount was not deducted in calculating taxable income: instead, the tax rates used in calculating your tax included an adjustment for the zero bracket amount. If you itemized your deductions, you only subtracted the amount by which your itemized deductions *exceeded* the zero bracket amount.

Under the new Act, as we said earlier, all deductions—either your itemized deductions or the standard deduction—are subtracted in calculating taxable income, and the tax tables no longer include the zero bracket adjustment.

Here's how the standard deduction will change in 1987 and 1988:

Status	Amount of Standard Deduction		
	1986	*1987*	*1988*
Single Person	$2,480	2,540	3,000
Married Filing Jointly	3,670	3,760	5,000
Married Filing Separately	1,835	1,880	2,500
Head of Household	2,480	2,540	4,400

As the table shows, the new, higher standard deduction does not take effect until 1988. The 1987 standard deduction represents only an inflation adjustment over the 1986 figures.

Elderly or Blind

However, an exception is made in the case of the elderly or blind. For the elderly and/or blind, the higher 1988 standard deduction takes effect in *1987*, together with other special adjustments. As we pointed out in Chapter 4, the additional personal exemptions that the old law gave to the elderly and/or blind are eliminated in the new law and replaced with additional standard deductions.

If you are single, and are age 65 or older or are blind, you are entitled to an additional standard deduction of $750 for each condition (maximum of $1,500). If you are married, you and your spouse are each entitled to an additional standard deduction of $600 for each condition (a maximum of $2,400 if both spouses are age 65 or over and blind). All these changes go into effect in 1987.

Where does this leave the person who is age 65 or older and/or blind? It will vary from case to case. For those who itemize deductions—as is true in many cases, especially where medical expenses are high—the increase in the standard deduction may not be of any help. The single individual who is age 70 and blind was entitled in 1986 to three personal exemptions totalling $3,240. In 1987, the same individual is entitled to a single personal exemption of $1,900. Progress sometimes seems to run in strange directions.

Dependent's Standard Deduction

As we said in Chapter 4, an individual who is taken as a dependent on someone else's tax return cannot claim the personal exemption on his/her own return, and also may not be able to take the full standard deduction. For such an individual, the standard deduction taken must be the *lesser* of (a) the usual standard deduction or (b) the amount of the individual's earned income, plus up to

$500 of unearned income. (So an individual in this status who has $2,000 of earned income in 1988 and $3,000 of unearned income will only be able to take a standard deduction of $2,500. With $3,000 of earned income and $10,000 of unearned income, the standard deduction would be the maximum $3,000.)

Under the old law, a dependent with unearned income was entitled to take the personal exemption but could not use any portion of his/her zero bracket amount to offset unearned income. Under the new law, the maximum amount of a dependent's unearned income that can be free of tax is reduced from approximately $1,080 (the 1985 personal exemption amount) to $500.

6

IF YOU DO NOT ITEMIZE

Under the prior law, a taxpayer who chose to take the standard deduction rather than itemizing was entitled to take several "adjustments" to reduce adjusted gross income. The new Act retains the following adjustments:

- IRA contributions (where permitted)
- Keogh contributions
- Alimony paid
- Penalty for early withdrawal of savings (imposed on some savings accounts if withdrawn before the maturity date)

The other adjustments under the prior law are now treated as follows under the new law:

The Two-Earner Deduction

The deduction for a married couple when both work is eliminated under the new law. See Chapter 7.

Moving Expenses

If you move because you change your job, certain of the moving expenses can still be deducted. But they will now have to be taken as an itemized deduction. See Chapter 11.

Employee Business Expenses

Under the old law, nonreimbursed business expenses, including an outside salesperson's expenses, could be deducted as an adjustment to income. Under the new law, these can only be taken as itemized deductions, and the deduction is subject to certain limitations. See Chapter 11.

7

MARRIAGE PENALTY

When it comes to taxes, it may not pay to be married.

Working married couples have frequently been penalized for their wedded state by paying higher federal income taxes than if they were single. That's the way the tax brackets have worked—and will continue to work under the new law.

Repeal of the Two-Earner Deduction

The prior law offset at least part of this so-called marriage penalty by allowing working couples a "two-earner" deduction if they filed a joint tax return. This deduction amounted to the lesser of $3,000 or 10% of the earned income of the spouse who earned the lower income.

The new tax law, with its reduced maximum tax liability of 28% or 33%, eliminates the two-earner deduction. This means that a working married couple, whether they file jointly or separately, may still pay more tax than their single counterparts.

Let's look at an example:

ILLUSTRATION OF THE "MARRIAGE PENALTY"*

Earnings	Married Filing Jointly	Single	Married Filing Separately
Spouse A earns $45,000	A + B pay $13,240	$ 8,900	$ 9,650
Spouse B earns $25,000		3,300	3,820
TOTAL TAX	$13,240 −12,200	$12,200	$13,470 −12,200
"Marriage Penalty"	$ 1,040		$ 1,270

*All amounts rounded to the nearest $10. Liabilities calculated based on 1988 tax rates. Table assumes standard deduction, no dependents, and wages as the sole source of income.　　　　　　　　　　*Source: Price Waterhouse*

8

STATE AND LOCAL TAXES

Under the old law, if you itemized, state and local income, sales, real estate, and personal property taxes were fully deductible.

No Sales Tax Deduction

After long debate, the congressional tax writers decided to retain most of these deductions. Under the new law, if you itemize your deductions rather than taking the standard deduction, you can still deduct state and local income, real estate and personal property taxes. But you can no longer take state and local *sales* taxes as a deduction. This change takes effect on January 1, 1987.

A Small Offset

But keep track of sales (or transfer) taxes paid on major items, especially on real estate. If you purchase property after January 1, 1987, any nondeductible state and local taxes you pay on the purchase may qualify to be added to the cost basis of the property. This could reduce your tax if you eventually sell the property at a profit. Moreover, in the case of residential real estate, as we shall see in Chapter 9, a higher cost basis will increase the amount of mortgage interest that you can deduct on your tax return.

9

MORTGAGE AND OTHER INTEREST DEDUCTIONS

One of the major changes made by the Tax Reform Bill of 1986 is the treatment of deductions for interest payments. "Consumer interest" payments, including interest on credit cards, automobile loans, personal loans, etc., will be phased out as a deduction. *But interest on a home mortgage is still generally deductible.* "Investment interest"—interest incurred to make or carry investments—will be deductible only within tighter limits than previously. Interest incurred in connection with a trade or business will remain generally deductible.

Mortgage Interest

Home ownership has always been part of the American dream and an important part of American politics. After much debate, the congressional tax writers decided to retain the deduction for mortgage interest (just as they decided to retain the deduction for state and local property taxes).

But there are restrictions. The deduction for "qualified housing interest" is limited to interest on debt taken against a taxpayer's *principal residence* or *second residence* only. Moreover, *the debt may not exceed the cost basis of the property*—the original purchase price plus the cost of any improvements.

But there is an intriguing exception to the cost basis rule—the debt can exceed this figure to the extent it is incurred for educational or medical expenses. (The educational expenses may include reasonable living expenses away from home for students from primary through graduate school.)

August 17, 1986

Also, *if you refinanced your mortgage before August 17, 1986*, the mortgage amount can be up to the *fair market value* of the property, and the interest will still be fully deductible, even if the fair market value exceeds the cost basis.

What Is a Residence?

If one of your homes, such as a vacation home, is rented out part of the time, mortgage interest will be fully deductible as "qualified residence interest" only if you use the home personally for the *greater* of (a) 14 days or (b) 10% of the number of days for which the home is rented out. Otherwise, the mortgage interest will be considered as an expense of the rental activity, and it will be deductible only against rental income or other "passive activity" income (see Chapters 18 and 19).

And the debt must be on a *residence*. This means that if you own land on which you hope some day to build a vacation home, any interest you pay on a loan against that land will not be deductible as long as no residence has yet been built on the land.

Cooperatives

Loans on cooperative residential apartments qualify for the interest deduction, even though they are not, technically speaking, mortgages on real estate.

Time-Sharing Interests

The interest paid on a loan to purchase a time-sharing interest in a vacation home is not deductible as "qualified residence interest" under the new Act, but must be treated either as investment interest or as nondeductible personal ("consumer") interest.

Your Cost Basis

Since the mortgage debt on which you can deduct interest will generally be limited to the original purchase price of your home plus the cost of any improvements, it becomes particularly important to keep careful track of the amount spent on improvements. If you bought your home for $80,000 and have since spent $4,000 for a finished basement and $8,000 for a new kitchen, your new cost basis will be $92,000 and, under the new Act, you can deduct interest paid on a mortgage loan of up to $92,000.

The burden of establishing the cost of home improvements is on the taxpayer, and we urge you to keep complete and accurate records of your actual expenditures. If you can't find receipts for home improvements made in the past, go back to the contractor or worker who did the work, and try to get a duplicate invoice or some other documentation of the costs.

State and Local Taxes

If you should pay (or have paid) any state or local tax on the purchase of your home, make sure that this cost is properly recorded (it should be reflected on your settlement sheet), since the tax can be included as part of your cost basis under the new law.

Refinancing Thoughts

Because mortgage interest remains tax-deductible while the deduction on consumer interest is being phased out, many people will undoubtedly borrow more on their mortgages, or through home equity lines of credit, in preference to incurring other kinds of debt. Certainly this seems logical. For example, in buying a home you might make the smallest possible down payment and take out the largest possible mortgage in order to have cash available for other purposes.

But remember the limits on interest deductibility described above. And even if you are within those limits, be careful about borrowing more than you need. Remember that when you borrow against your home, your home is at stake.

When refinancing or taking out a home equity loan, be sure that you are clear about the actual cost of the refinancing. And if you are borrowing at an adjustable interest rate, consider how your loan payments may escalate if interest rates rise. See the No-Nonsense Real Estate Guide, *Refinancing Your Mortgage*.

Remember, too, that because of the general drop in tax rates, the mortgage interest deduction—like all other deductions—will be worth less in dollars than it used to be. If you paid $1,000 of mortgage interest in 1986, and were in the 50% tax bracket, the deduction saved you $500 in cash. In 1988, if you are in the 28% bracket, the same deduction will save you only $280.

The Educational-Medical Exception

What if you want to refinance your mortgage for more than your cost basis, and use the excess for educational or medical expenses? Here's an example of how the figures might possibly work out:

Let's say that your original home purchase price was $65,000 and that you have added $10,000 in improvements, so that your basis is $75,000. Let's also assume that your mortgage has been paid down to a point where the principal balance is now $40,000; your home has appreciated in value and is now worth $140,000; and you can refinance your mortgage, taking out a new mortgage for $120,000. This gives you $80,000 of new cash, of which $20,000 will be used for college expenses for your two children. Since the size of the mortgage exceeds your cost basis by $45,000 ($120,000 minus the cost basis of $75,000), and since you will spend $20,000 on education expenses, presumably you can deduct the interest on $95,000 of the mortgage, though not on the total $120,000.

The possibilities of abuse are obvious, and the Internal Revenue Service (IRS) will undoubtedly issue detailed rules on this subject in time. We see major accounting problems arising out of these provisions, and suggest that you keep accurate and detailed records of expenses if you intend to qualify for the additional education or medical expense mortgage deduction.

Consumer Interest

Under previous law, any interest you paid on borrowings was deductible. You could, for example, deduct the interest you paid on your automobile loan, your home mortgage, your credit cards, bank loans, education loans, etc.

As we said at the beginning of this chapter, the new Act dramatically changes the rules regarding interest expense deductions. "Consumer interest" that you pay on car loans, education loans, loans to pay taxes, etc. will be phased out completely as a deduction over a 5-year period.

Consumer or personal interest is defined to include generally any interest you pay that is *not* classified as mortgage interest, investment interest, interest incurred in a trade or business, or interest incurred in a "passive activity" type investment (see Chapter 18).

Incidentally, if you underpay your estimated tax, and owe interest to the IRS on the underpayments, that interest will be treated as consumer interest and will not be deductible.

Timing of the Phase-out

The schedule for phasing out the consumer interest deduction is as follows:

Year	Portion of Interest Deductible
1986	100%
1987	65%
1988	40%
1989	20%
1990	10%
1991 and after	0%

Investment Interest

Investment interest—the interest you pay on borrowings to buy or carry securities or other investments—is treated under separate rules described in Chapter 16.

Business Interest

Interest incurred in a trade or business remains, in general, fully deductible, like most other business expenses.

10

CHARITABLE CONTRIBUTIONS AND MEDICAL EXPENSES

Beginning in 1987, the rules on deductions for charitable contributions and medical expenses will be changed.

Charitable Contributions

The old law allowed charitable contributions to be deducted in 1986 whether or not you itemized, but removed that tax break for 1987. The new law holds to that schedule: beginning in 1987, only those who itemize deductions can deduct charitable contributions.

Although some deductions for travel expenses are eliminated under the new law, travel expense may be deductible if you travel as a service for a charitable institution, provided there is no significant element of personal pleasure involved.

Medical Expenses

The previous law allowed medical expenses to be deducted by taxpayers who itemized, but only to the extent that the expenses exceeded 5% of adjusted gross income (AGI). This was often referred to as the "5% floor" under medical expenses. The new law raises the floor to 7.5% of AGI. This means that beginning in 1987, only those medical expenses which exceed 7.5% of your AGI can be deducted.

Handicapped Barriers

The new law makes special provision so that the elimination of structural barriers in the home of a person who is handicapped will be included as a deductible medical expense.

11

EMPLOYEE AND OTHER DEDUCTIONS AND CREDITS

For taxpayers who itemized, there have always been a wide range of possible miscellaneous deductions, including any nonreimbursed business expenses that were not deducted previously in arriving at adjusted gross income. The Tax Reform Act of 1986 provides that, beginning in 1987, most of these deductions will be lumped together, and the total will only be deductible to the extent that it exceeds 2% of adjusted gross income (AGI).

Obviously, it will be important to distinguish between the deductions that are subject to the 2% floor and those that are not.

Moving Expenses

If you move because of a job change, a certain amount of moving expenses may be deductible. Previously, these expenses were an above-the-line adjustment, deductible in arriving at adjusted gross income, with the deduction available even to taxpayers who did not itemize. Under the new law, moving expenses can be taken only as an itemized deduction, but they are *not* subject to the 2% floor.

Other Exceptions to the 2% Floor

There are only a handful of other miscellaneous deductions not subject to the 2% floor. Among the more important of these are certain work-related expenses of handicapped employees. Also, certain special investment expenses are deductible without reference to the floor. And you can deduct all your gambling losses—but only up to the amount of the gambling winnings you report.

Other Business Expenses

Most nonreimbursed employee business expenses are now deductible only as itemized deductions, and generally subject to the 2% floor. This can include a wide range of items—some examples are outside salesperson's expenses, union and professional dues, tools, uniforms, business publications, employment agency fees, etc.

A tip: Employees who regularly incur nonreimbursed expenses should consider discussing the possibility of reimbursement with their employer, even in lieu of additional salary. If the expenses are not fully deductible, the reimbursement may work out better than salary on an after-tax basis.

Business Meals and Entertainment

Under the old tax law, business meals and entertainment were fully deductible as a business expense, with certain restrictions. The new law provides that beginning in 1987, only 80% of qualified business meal and entertainment expenses are deductible (see Chapter 20). For an employee with nonreimbursed expenses of this type, only 80% of the total qualifies for a deduction, and this 80% amount is then subject to the 2% floor.

Home Office Deduction

Deductions for the business use of a home have always been a sensitive issue for both employees and self-employed business people. The new law makes a change by providing that if an employer rents space in the home of an employee, no deduction will be allowed. This rule is extended to independent contractors, who will be treated as employees for this provision.

Other Miscellaneous Deductions

The new law makes a few changes in other popular miscellaneous deductions. Travel for educational purposes no longer will be deductible. Travel expenses incurred to attend a meeting or convention on investments also are ruled out.

Note for all taxpayers: the fee you pay to a tax return preparer is still deductible, but subject to the 2% floor.

Casualty Losses

The old law permitted a deduction for nonbusiness casualty losses—as from storm, fire, automobile accidents, etc.—to the extent the loss exceeded 10% of adjusted gross income. The new law adds a requirement that if the loss is covered by insurance, the deduction can only be taken if the taxpayer files a claim against his/her insurance company in a timely manner. (Any insurance recovery is subtracted in calculating the deductible loss.)

Performing Artists

The new law specifies that actors, musicians and other performing artists even though they are technically *employees* of producers or other employers when they are working, are to be treated as *independent contractors* if they meet three tests: (1) the taxpayer-performer must have two or more work-related jobs during the year, (2) the taxpayer's work-related expenses must be greater than 10% of gross income, and (3) his/her adjusted gross income before deducting work-related expenses must not exceed $16,000. If these three tests are met, the performer will be treated as an independent contractor, eligible to deduct all business expenses, rather than as an employee, and the 2% deduction floor will not apply.

Deductions and Credits

A tax *deduction* reduces taxable income and saves tax, depending on the taxpayer's bracket; a tax *credit* reduces the tax directly. For a taxpayer in the 28% bracket, a $100 deduction saves $28 of tax, but a $100 credit saves $100 of tax.

Most tax credits are "nonrefundable": if the credit is greater than your tax, the tax is eliminated and the excess amount of the credit is ignored. But certain credits, including the earned income credit noted below, are "refundable": if the credit is greater than your tax, the IRS actually pays you the difference.

Child and Dependent Care Credit

The new tax law maintains the existing child and dependent care credit (a nonrefundable credit). If you pay someone to care for a dependent child under 15 or a disabled spouse or dependent while you work or look for work, and if you meet various requirements, you may be entitled to a credit of up to $720 for one dependent, or up to $1,440 if more than one. The actual amount of the credit will vary depending on your adjusted gross income and the amount you have paid in care expense.

Credit for the Elderly

The new tax law maintains the existing credit for the elderly and disabled (a nonrefundable credit). For those with incomes under certain limits, this credit may be up to $1,125 if a taxpayer or spouse is 65 or older, or is under 65 and has retired on permanent and total disability.

Earned Income Credit

The new tax law *increases* this credit. The old law allowed low-income families with one or more children, and with income under $11,000, a credit of up to $550 if certain requirements were met. The new law increases the maximum credit to $800, beginning in 1987, and raises the income limits. This is a *refundable* credit—if the credit exceeds the tax owed, the IRS mails out a check for the difference.

Political Contributions

The old law provided a tax *credit* of up to $50 ($100 on a joint return) against certain political contributions. The new law eliminates the credit, beginning in 1987.

12

A *NO-NONSENSE* LOOK AT 1987

1987 may be a confusing year for your tax return. Some of the provisions of the new law go into full effect in 1987, while others are introduced only in a "blended" or phased-in state, and still others are not introduced at all until 1988 or later.

Depending on the deductions they are accustomed to taking, some taxpayers may find 1987 a disappointing year. Some deductions will be eliminated entirely, while the drop in tax rates will go only part way.

To help reduce the confusion, this chapter summarizes some of the 1987 provisions detailed elsewhere in this book. We think the need for clarification justifies the repetition.

Tax Brackets

As noted in Chapter 2, 1987 represents a blended year for tax brackets. The many brackets of the old law are combined with the two brackets of the future to produce the following 1987 tax rates:

	Taxable Income		1987 Tax Rate
Married Filing Jointly	*Single*	*Head of Household*	
$0 – 3,000	$0 – 1,800	$0 – 2,500	**11%**
3,000 – 28,000	1,800 – 16,800	2,500 – 23,000	**15%**
28,000 – 45,000	16,800 – 27,000	23,000 – 38,000	**28%**
45,000 – 90,000	27,000 – 54,000	38,000 – 80,000	**35%**
over 90,000	over 54,000	over 80,000	**38.5%**

Capital Gains

Long-term capital gains will be taxed at the above rates in 1987, but with a maximum rate of 28%. Short-term capital gains will be taxed completely at the above rates. See Chapter 16.

Dividend Exclusion

The dividend exclusion will no longer apply in 1987. See Chapter 16.

Personal Exemption

The 1987 personal exemption will be $1,900 per person. See Chapter 4.

Standard Deduction

In 1987, the standard deduction will be as follows:

Status	Standard Deduction
Single Person	$2,540
Married Filing Jointly	3,760
Married Filing Separately	1,880
Head of Household	2,540

An Important Note for Elderly or Blind Taxpayers

The additional personal exemptions for elderly and/or blind taxpayers are eliminated in 1987. However, elderly and/or blind taxpayers may take the increased 1988 standard deduction as well as the $600 (if married) or $750 (if single) over-65 or blind addition to the standard deduction in 1987, a year before these deductions apply to the rest of the population. See Chapter 5.

Marriage Penalty (Two-Earner Deduction)

The two-earner deduction is eliminated beginning in 1987. See Chapter 7.

State and Local Taxes

State and local income, property, and school taxes remain deductible under the new law.

State and local sales taxes will no longer be deductible beginning in 1987. See Chapter 8.

Interest Deductions

Interest on mortgages on your primary and secondary residences remains basically deductible under the new law, with certain limitations. Deductions for personal or "consumer" interest will be phased out over five years, with 65% of such interest deductible in 1987. Tighter limitations on investment interest deductions are phased in over five years. See Chapters 9 and 16.

Nonreimbursed Employee Business Expenses

All nonreimbursed employee business-related expenses, such as union and professional dues, business periodicals, uniform expense, outside salesperson's expense, etc., will only be deductible as itemized deductions subject to a floor of 2% of adjusted gross income. See Chapter 11.

Charitable Contributions

Contributions to charity will only be deductible in 1987 and thereafter by taxpayers who itemize. See Chapter 10.

Medical Expenses

Medical expenses will only be deductible in 1987 and after if they exceed a floor of 7.5% of adjusted gross income. See Chapter 10.

Unemployment Compensation

Beginning in 1987, unemployment compensation will be fully taxable.

IRAs

Tax deductions for IRA contributions are greatly curtailed in 1987. However, contributions for 1986 can be made until April 15, 1987, under the old rules. See Chapter 13.

401(k)

Elective contributions to 401(k) plans are limited to $7,000 in 1987 and thereafter. See Chapter 14.

Planning Your Deductions

Since 1987 tax rates are higher than 1988, there will be an extra advantage to paying any deductible expenses, such as state income taxes and charitable contributions, before the end of 1987 rather than waiting until 1988.

PART III
HOW THE NEW
TAX LAW AFFECTS
YOUR RETIREMENT

13

IRAs

Does the new tax law take away your IRA? No, it doesn't. But for millions of taxpayers, the law makes the IRA considerably less attractive than it was before.

Under the old law, if you worked for a living, you could have put up to $2,000 annually in an Individual Retirement Account (IRA) and taken a full tax deduction for the amount contributed. Under the new law, that's still assured *only if you don't actively participate in any other retirement plan*. If you *do* participate in an employer's retirement plan, the following income limitations apply:

—If you are single and your adjusted gross income (calculated *before* the IRA deduction) is less than $25,000 (or $40,000 for a married couple filing jointly), you can make an IRA contribution of up to $2,000 and take a full tax deduction, just as you did before.

—If you are single and your adjusted gross income (before the IRA deduction) is over $35,000 (or $50,000 for a couple filing jointly), you can still put the money in an IRA, but *none* of the contribution is tax-deductible.

—In the transition range—$25,000-35,000 of adjusted gross income for an individual, or $40,000-50,000 for a married couple—the tax deduction drops by $200 for each additional $1,000 of adjusted gross income.

What if only one spouse is covered by an employer retirement plan? That depends. If the couple file a joint return, both spouses become subject to the limited-deductibility rules. But if they file separate returns, each spouse is treated separately, and any plan participation by one does not affect the other. The problem here (apart from other possibly adverse effects of filing separate returns) is that for married persons filing separately and

43

participating in an employer plan, the deduction phases out between $0 and $10,000 of adjusted gross income (before the IRA deduction). So for married persons filing separately, the deduction is available only to a spouse who does not participate in an employer plan or who has very low income.

If any of the limitations are likely to affect you, you should ask your company personnel office whether you are considered an "active participant" in an employer retirement plan. The definition of "active participant" usually is obvious, but there are special borderline cases.

The Silver Lining

But don't give up on your IRA—even if you (and your spouse, if married) are covered by another plan, and are at an income level where you lose the tax deduction. Since the IRA was made widely available in 1982, it has carried two tremendous advantages: (1) contributions have been tax-deductible, and (2) money in an IRA *earns and compounds tax-free*.

Many people have opened IRAs mainly for the tax deduction. But over the long term, the biggest benefits of an IRA are likely to come from the *tax-free compounding*. And the new law leaves this great advantage intact.

Before we say more about this advantage, let's review the basic IRA rules and how they stand in light of the new law.

Some IRA Basics

Anyone with *earned* income can have an IRA. Income from dividends, interest, rent, pensions, etc. is classified as "unearned" income and can't be the basis for an IRA contribution; but since 1985, *alimony* has qualified as earned income for IRA purposes.

You can contribute up to $2,000 or 100% of your earned income, whichever is less, to an IRA. You have flexibility: you can contribute $2,000 each year, or less, or nothing at all. Contributions for a given year can be made up until April 15 of the following year.

If both spouses work, each can have a separate IRA, and each can contribute up to the legal limit. The new law doesn't interfere with the concept of separate IRAs; but, as noted above, the tax deduction for contributions to both IRAs will be limited if either spouse is covered by a company retirement plan and they file a joint return.

Under the old law, if one spouse had no earned income at all, a *spousal IRA* could be set up for that spouse, and the total contributed to the couple's two IRAs could be up to $2,250. The new law permits this even if the second spouse has some earned income, and makes the revision effective beginning with 1986; but note that if the second spouse has more than $250 of earned income, the couple can contribute a greater total by having the second spouse open a regular IRA.

You can still have an IRA at as early an age as you wish, and you still are not allowed to contribute in the year in which you reach age $70\frac{1}{2}$, or later. There has been a slight change in the time when you must begin taking withdrawals: previously it was in the calendar year when you reached age $70\frac{1}{2}$; now you don't need to begin withdrawing until April 1 of the year following that calendar year.

While distributions from an IRA will generally continue to be taxed as ordinary income, the new law provides for an adjustment if you make nondeductible contributions to your IRA. A part of your withdrawals, equal to the total dollar amount of those nondeductible contributions, will be withdrawn without tax; but the accumulated *earnings* on those contributions will be taxed. Under rules still to be refined, any distribution will include a nontaxable percentage equal to the proportion that your past nondeductible contributions bear to the total current value of your IRA. (Obviously, it will be important to distinguish deductible from nondeductible contributions and to keep adequate records.)

There is still a special penalty tax of 10% (in addition to ordinary income tax) payable on amounts you withdraw from an IRA before age $59\frac{1}{2}$. The major exceptions are withdrawals because of death or disability; also, any portion of your withdrawals that represents past *nondeductible* contributions is not subject to the penalty.

One more change, this time on a lighter note: the old law prohibited an IRA from investing in "collectibles," a term that includes precious metals. But the new law permits an IRA to invest in gold or silver coins issued by the U.S. government.

All these changes, except with respect to the spousal IRA, take effect in 1987. But *IRA contributions for 1986 will continue to be permitted through April 15, 1987 under the old 1986 rules.*

Your IRA Decisions

For many people, the IRA will continue to be a key element in retirement planning. If you are still eligible to make deductible contributions, the IRA offers a remarkable opportunity to enjoy these deductions together with the benefits of tax-free compounding. It is literally too good an opportunity to pass up, unless your job situation lets you get comparable benefits from a Keogh, 401(k), or other retirement plan.

What if you are not eligible for the tax deduction? Obviously, if you can make tax-deductible contributions to a Keogh plan or 401(k) plan, either plan will give you an edge over an IRA. But if you don't have those options, the IRA can still be highly attractive, especially if you are well below age 70 and have several years to enjoy the advantage of tax-free compounding.

Tax-Free Compounding

Here are two examples of how that advantage works. We've assumed a single $2,000 investment in an IRA, growing in one case at a 10% compound annual rate and in the other case at 15%. We've also assumed that the owner is in the 28% tax bracket, so that the $2,000 invested the same way outside the IRA would compound at rates of 7.2% and 10.8%, respectively, after paying tax on each year's earnings:

IRA vs. NON-IRA INVESTMENTS

Value at End of Year	10% Growth Rate		15% Growth Rate	
	In IRA	Outside IRA	In IRA	Outside IRA
1 Year	$ 2,200	$ 2,144	$ 2,300	$ 2,216
5 Years	3,221	2,831	4,023	3,340
10 Years	5,187	4,008	8,091	5,577
15 Years	8,354	5,675	16,274	9,314
20 Years	13,455	8,034	32,733	15,553
30 Years	34,899	16,102	132,423	43,373
40 Years	90,518	32,272	535,727	120,954

In the 10%–7.2% example, you could take the IRA money out after 20 years, pay tax on it at 28% (on all but your original $2,000), and still be left with $10,248— more than the $8,034 you would have accumulated outside the IRA. After 30 years, the comparison would be $25,687 against $16,102. In the 15%–10.8% example, the comparison is $24,128 against $15,553 after 20 years, and $95,905 against $43,373 after 30 years.

Flexibility and Control

Tax-free compounding isn't the only advantage. An IRA is under your own control, and highly flexible. You can vary your contributions; you can easily switch from one investment to another; and you have considerable latitude as to just when you take the money out.

Of course, if you are under age 59¹/₂, you should think twice (or three times) about putting money in an IRA that you think you may need in the near future. The 10% penalty tax does mean that you are mildly "locked in." But as the table above shows, once the money has been in the plan for several years, the extra growth from the tax deferral should outweigh the impact of the penalty tax, if you should have to take the money out.

What's the hitch? There's one uncertainty that can't be resolved at this point. IRA distributions have always been taxed as ordinary income, with none of the breaks on lump-sum distributions that have been enjoyed by other types of retirement plans. Right now, with tax rates coming down, this disadvantage doesn't seem too important. But what if tax rates rise in the future, as could well happen? The value of your IRA might be less at retirement than you had projected. It's a problem worth thinking about; but we don't think it should prevent you from putting the maximum you can in an IRA and letting the benefits of compounding improve your retirement.

14

401(k) AND OTHER
COMPANY PLANS

The Tax Reform Act of 1986 makes a wide range of changes in the rules covering company-sponsored retirement plans. Some of the changes are intended to make sure that more employees are included and treated fairly under company retirement plans, with tighter limits on the advantages permitted to higher-paid employees and generally stricter nondiscrimination rules. Some privileges under the plans have been curtailed. At the very top end of the scale, there is tougher tax treatment when benefits are finally withdrawn.

401(k) Plans and Elective Contributions

The most publicized change is the reduction in the maximum amount an employee can direct on a tax-deferred basis into a 401(k) plan, from $30,000 previously to $7,000 beginning in 1987. The *total* that can be contributed to such a plan can still be as high as $30,000 annually—but now, to reach that maximum, $23,000 would have to come from the employer.

Obviously, the new limitation will only affect certain highly paid employees. The main structure of 401(k) plans—also termed "salary reduction" or "cash or deferred" plans—remains intact. Under these plans, an employee has the option of having part of his or her pay directed into the plan, rather than being paid out as cash wages or salary, and no income tax is paid on the amount so contributed.

A 401(k) plan is often set up in combination with a regular profit-sharing arrangement, and in some cases the company may match part or all of the employee contribution on some basis. The plans have grown rapidly in popularity. Now, with IRA deductions curtailed or eliminated for many employees, there will be more pressure on employers to adopt 401(k) plans or to expand existing plans.

A 401(k) plan gives you somewhat less flexibility and individual control than an IRA, but there are offsetting advantages. For example, you can borrow from a 401(k) plan, but not from an IRA. Since you may be able to put as much as $7,000 annually into a 401(k) plan, the tax-free compounding possibilities are tremendous.

403(b) Plans

The limits on elective contributions under "403(b)" plans—the tax-sheltered annuity programs available to employees of many schools and other nonprofit institutions—also will be curtailed under the new law. Beginning in 1987, the maximum elective employee contribution will be limited to $9,500 annually, although the maximum total contribution (including amounts contributed by the employer) is still $30,000.

SEP-IRA Plans

For firms with not over 25 employees, the new law opens a new option for elective tax-deferred contributions by creating a variation of the existing "simplified employee pension plan," or SEP-IRA—a profit-sharing plan under which the employer contributes directly to special IRA-type retirement accounts set up for each covered employee. Now there will be "salary reduction simplified employee pensions" to which an employee can contribute as much as $7,000 annually tax-deferred, comparable to a 401(k) plan.

Retirement Plan Benefits

The new law makes many major changes in the ways retirement plan *benefits* will be paid and taxed.

When Must Distributions Begin?

An individual covered under any type of retirement plan (including IRAs) will have to begin to take distributions by April 1 of the year following the year in which he or she reaches age 70½, even if he or she is still working. Under a special transition rule, an employee who reaches age 70½ before 1988 may be able to defer benefits until actual retirement.

Lump Sum Distributions

The tax treatment of *lump sum distributions* from retirement plans other than IRAs is changed by the new law. Under the old law, lump sum pension distributions were entitled to a tax break called 10-year forward averaging—allowing distributions to be taxed as if spread out over 10 years, with no other income included. Moreover, if you had participated in a plan before 1974, part of your lump sum distribution could receive long-term capital gains treatment. Under the new law, these breaks are replaced by *5-year* forward averaging—and this is a one-time choice that can only be made after age 59½.

Two special transition rules help people who are already approaching retirement. If you reached age 50 before 1986, you will retain the option of having a lump sum distribution taxed under the old rules and using 1986 tax rates. (But beware of *any* distribution before age 59½—see below.) And for other plan participants, the phase-out of the capital gains treatment of certain amounts will be gradual, taking place over six years.

Note that there are favorable ways of spreading out payments over your lifetime if you don't want to be taxed on a lump sum distribution. In some cases, taking a lump sum distribution and rolling it over into a "rollover" IRA may be the best way to manage your benefit payments. The money is taxed only as it is withdrawn from the IRA.

Defined Benefit Maximum

The maximum annual retirement benefit that can be paid under a defined benefit plan is still $90,000. However, there are now stricter rules cutting back this maximum on a sliding scale for retirement before age 65, and for individuals who have less than 10 years of plan participation.

Excise Tax on Large Distributions

Individuals who receive very large retirement plan distributions will be hit hard by a *special 15% excise tax on "excess retirement distributions."* If an individual receives distributions totalling more than $112,500 in a given year from all retirement plans taken together (including IRAs), the excess above $112,500 is subject to the 15% tax, in addition to all other income taxes. For a lump sum distribution, the tax applies to any amount over $562,500. (The dollar amounts will be adjusted upward for inflation.) However, the tax will be modified to the extent that the benefits were accumulated before August 1, 1986.

The 3-Year Rule

Under the old law, individuals who had contributed partially to their own pensions or annuities were allowed in many cases to take the first three years of periodic benefits tax-free, representing the amounts they had originally contributed; after the three years, all benefits were taxable. The new law requires that the nontaxable portion of benefits be prorated over the whole life of the pension or annuity.

Early Withdrawals

The new law tightens the rules on early distributions from retirement plans. Generally, all distributions from plans before age 59½ will be subject to a 10% penalty tax, in addition to regular taxes (as has been true in the past for IRAs and certain other cases). The penalty applies not only to withdrawals from IRAs and qualified plans (including 401(k) plans), but also to withdrawals from tax-sheltered annuities and deferred annuity contracts. However, the penalty tax does *not* apply to (1) amounts originally attributable to an employee's own after-tax contributions; (2) a scheduled series of periodic payments over the lifetime of an employee, or over the joint lives of an employee and beneficiary; (3) distributions to an employee who reaches age 55 and meets a plan's technical requirements for early retirement; (4) distributions on account of disability or death; (5) distributions used to pay deductible medical expenses (this exception does not apply to an IRA); (6) certain distributions from an employee stock ownership plan.

Hardship Withdrawals

The rules on *hardship withdrawals* are tightened under the new law. Beginning in 1988, hardship withdrawals from a 401(k) plan can only be made from an individual's elective contributions, not from other amounts in the plan.

Loans from Retirement Plans

Loans of up to $50,000 from retirement plans are still permitted, but under tighter rules beginning January 1, 1987. The *interest* paid on such loans taken out before 1987 is subject to the general rules on interest deductions explained in Chapter 9. On loans taken out beginning January 1, 1987, the interest deduction rules are tightened, and no deduction at all is permitted on loans to "key employees."

For Greater Fairness

As mentioned above, the new tax law aims at wider coverage and greater fairness in retirement plans. These provisions may have little to do with your individual tax return, but could affect you significantly. (They generally take full effect in 1989.) The following sections describe certain of these new provisions.

Vesting

The rules have been changed on *vesting*—the process by which your retirement benefits become attached to you so that you can't lose them even if you leave your job. Under the old law, an employer had to give you full vesting by your 10th year, or else phase in your rights between your 5th and 15th year. The new law requires either full vesting by the 5th year, or a phase-in between the 3rd and 7th year. This change should greatly reduce the loss of pension benefits through job switching. As of January 1, 1989, if you have been in a company pension plan for 5 years, you should be at least partially vested.

Integration with Social Security

Some retirement plans are *integrated with Social Security*. Since the plan concentrates on benefit ranges not covered by Social Security, the result is relatively higher contributions for higher-paid employees, and relatively lower contributions for lower-paid employees. The new law narrows the permitted difference in contributions between the two groups.

Employee Stock Ownership Plans

An employee stock ownership plan (ESOP) is a stock bonus plan, sometimes combined with a money purchase pension plan, under which stock of the employer is held for the benefit of employees. The new tax law makes various changes in the tax treatment of these plans from the standpoint of employers. It also encourages more diversification of investments in the plan, especially for an employee approaching retirement age, and it gives a tax break to the estate of a plan participant who dies.

Incentive Stock Options

Incentive stock options (ISOs) are a popular way of giving deferred compensation to executives. Generally, the employee is not taxed when the ISO is granted or when it is exercised to buy stock, but he or she recognizes taxable gain whenever the stock is sold. The new law gives more flexibility to ISOs by removing a previous requirement that the ISOs be exercised in the order granted; now, the employee can first exercise those options that provide the lowest purchase price on the stock. Also, a company can now grant an individual more than $100,000 in ISOs in a given year, as long as not more than $100,000 can be *exercised* in a given year.

The elimination of the special tax break on capital gains removes one advantage of ISOs, but does not change their general attractiveness. However, note that exercise of an ISO gives rise to a preference item in calculating a possible alternative minimum tax (see Chapter 21).

Health and Other Fringe Benefits

The Act takes the same approach for *health and other fringe benefit plans* as for retirement plans. Beginning in 1989, less discrimination in favor of highly paid employees will be permitted, and lower-paid employees might find their benefits improved in many cases as a result.

15

KEOGH PLANS

If you are a self-employed businessperson or professional—or anyone with part-time earnings from self-employment—the Tax Reform Act of 1986 continues to give you major opportunities for retirement saving. As we saw in the previous chapter, the law makes many changes in the rules for retirement plans. But the basic maximum benefits remain largely the same as before.

If You Have Employees

The tax-deductible contributions to a self-employed retirement plan (popularly known as Keogh plans) can be very large, and the money in the plan earns and compounds tax-free. But if you have set up a Keogh plan and *have employees*, the employees must be included in the plan on a specific schedule, and it is essential to confer with your accountant and/or attorney to make sure that you are following the rules correctly, including the new rules introduced by the 1986 tax law.

The Basic Choices

The rules on Keogh plans, and particularly on Keogh plan *contributions*, were greatly liberalized in 1984. Since many self-employed persons have not taken advantage of all the possibilities, let us point out that there are three major types of Keogh plans available:

1. A *profit-sharing* plan, under which a self-employed person can contribute up to 13.043% of earned income or $30,000, whichever is less. The great advantage is flexibility. The owner (or partners, if it is a partnership) can decide each year how much to

contribute, but any covered employees must receive contributions at the same base rate (unless the plan is integrated with Social Security—see Chapter 14).

2. A *money purchase pension plan*. The self-employed person can contribute up to 20% of earned income or $30,000, whichever is less; but whatever percentage rate is chosen, contributions must be made for employees each year at that rate (unless the plan is integrated with Social Security).

3. A *defined benefit pension plan*, under which contributions are calculated to provide a specific level of annual retirement income. The $30,000 annual limit doesn't apply, and for someone who starts such a plan close to retirement age, tax-deductible contributions can sometimes be as high as 100% of self-employed income.

Changes to Consider

The Tax Reform Act of 1986 did not change the basic contribution rules for Keogh plans summarized above, and some of the new restrictions described in the previous chapter had already been in effect for Keogh plans. But a few of the law's changes could be of great significance to anyone with a Keogh plan, especially if large amounts are being contributed.

In particular, consider (a) the change in tax treatment of lump-sum distributions and (b) the 15% excise tax on "excess distributions" (that is, on very large distributions). In view of the general lowering of tax rates, each of these changes is probably bearable. But is it worth making plan contributions now, and saving 28% or 33% of the contribution through tax deductions, only to be hit with possibly higher taxes when the plan eventually pays you benefits?

There's no clear answer. The longer the money will be in the plan, the more you will benefit from tax-free compounding. If you are getting close to retirement, and your plan is already large, careful calculations are needed, and you should by all means consult with your tax advisor.

PART IV
THE NEW TAX BILL
AND YOUR
INVESTMENTS

16

NEW RULES FOR INVESTORS

The Tax Reform Act of 1986 makes far-reaching changes for investors.

The New Capital Gain Rules

Under the old law, only 40% of net long-term capital gains—gains on securities or other property held more than six months—was taxed as income; the other 60% was excluded. The maximum effective tax on long-term gains, for an investor in the top 50% bracket, was only 20% (i.e., 50% of 40%). Investors in lower brackets paid proportionately less.

Net short-term gains—gains on property held six months or less—were fully taxed, like all other forms of income. (Despite the difference in tax rates, net long-term *losses* could be offset dollar for dollar against net short-term *gains*, and vice versa.)

Capital Gain Tax Rates

Beginning in 1988, net long-term gains will be taxed at the same rates as all other types of income—at 15% or 28% or, for those in the range subject to the 5% surtax, at 33%.

For 1987, long-term gains will be taxed basically like other income, but a special transition rule provides that the rate will not exceed 28%.

Net Capital Losses

The handling of net capital losses has been adapted to the new rules. Beginning in 1987, if you have a net capital loss in any year, whether long-term or short-term, up to

$3,000 of the loss can be deducted against other types of income; any loss above $3,000 can be carried forward indefinitely and either deducted in full against future capital gains, or deducted against other income at the rate of $3,000 per year. The distinction between long-term losses and short-term losses will have no practical importance.

(Under the old law, only 50% of *long-term* losses could be used to offset ordinary income. So it took $6,000 of long-term losses to provide the maximum $3,000 deduction against ordinary income, and tax loss carryforwards had to be specifically identified as long-term or short-term. This "discount" on deducting long-term losses against ordinary income now disappears.)

Futures Contracts and Options

By eliminating the distinction between long-term and short-term gains, the new law nullifies the special treatment given to futures contracts, index options, and certain other options. Previously, any gain or loss on these items was taxed 60% as long-term gain or loss and 40% as short-term gain or loss, no matter how short the holding period. The difference in rates between long- and short-term will be small in 1987 and nonexistent in 1988.

Dividend Exclusion

Under the old law, the first $100 of dividends ($200 for a married couple filing jointly) could generally be excluded from income, depending on the type of dividend. The new law eliminates the dividend exclusion.

Investment Interest

Investment interest is the interest you pay on money borrowed to buy or carry investment property, such as stocks or bonds. The new tax law tightens the restrictions on the amount of investment interest you can deduct for tax purposes.

The law requires that you match investment *interest* against investment *income* (interest, dividends, rents, etc.). Under the old law, the amount of investment interest you could deduct was limited to the amount of your net investment income, *plus $10,000*. Under the new law, the deduction is limited simply to the amount of your net investment income; the $10,000 additional allowance will be phased out over 5 years, beginning in 1987.

Investment Income Defined

"Investment income" previously included dividends, interest, rents, royalties and net short-term capital gains. Under the new law, net long-term capital gains also are included. "Net investment income," for purposes of the rule, is investment income minus investment expenses; and investment expenses are all the expenses connected with the production of investment income, other than interest.

Margin Borrowings

Probably the most common type of investment interest is interest paid to a brokerage firm on a margin account used to buy and hold securities. If you borrow on margin, it's important to track the relationship between the interest you pay and the investment income of various types that you earn. If you borrow on margin for noninvestment purposes, the interest you pay is no longer investment interest, but is subject to the different rules on "consumer interest." (See Chapter 9.)

Passive Activities

As we shall see in Chapter 18, the new law sets up a whole new category of "passive activities" intended to control and largely eliminate traditional "tax shelter" deductions. Under the new rules, interest expense in connection with "passive" activities, such as tax shelters, is treated separately and is not classified as investment interest. However, a borrowing to make an investment in a limited partnership may be classified as investment interest.

Real Estate Renting and Leasing

Real estate renting and leasing activities, and other renting and leasing activities, are now generally classified as passive activities. So interest paid in connection with these activities also is dealt with under the passive activity rules, and is not considered investment interest.

A warning: despite the basic separation of "passive activities" under the new Act, there are certain areas where the results of passive activities can become intertwined with the results of certain investment activities. If you are involved in any "passive activity," you should certainly consult an accountant to decide on the best steps to take under the new rules.

Tax-Exempt Bonds

The tax treatment of municipal bonds was a subject of great speculation and debate as the Tax Reform Act of 1986 was being written. In its final form, the Act leaves investors a wide range of tax-exempt bonds available for investment. Of course, the general reduction in tax brackets means that the advantage of the tax exemption is less than it used to be.

Under the law, the interest on municipal bonds issued before August 8, 1986 will continue to be tax-free. For bonds issued on August 8, 1986 or later, distinctions must be made:

- Interest on bonds issued by state and local governments to finance regular government operations and services will remain completely free from federal income tax.

- Interest on certain "private purpose" municipal bonds will be exempt from regular tax but will be a "tax preference" item subject to the alternative minimum tax. (See Chapter 21.)

- Interest on other "private purpose" bonds will be completely taxable.

Obviously, if you buy municipal bonds, you will need to be sure just which type you are buying. If you are subject to the alternative minimum tax, you will want to avoid bonds that fall under that tax. But because of that disadvantage, those bonds may sell at lower prices and higher yields than the fully tax-exempt bonds, and may at times offer opportunities to investors *not* subject to the alternative minimum tax.

Taxable Equivalent Yields

What advantages do tax-exempts provide at the tax brackets introduced under the new law? The following table of "taxable equivalent yields" shows the *taxable yields* that you would have to earn, at different tax brackets, to equal a given *tax-exempt* yield:

TABLE OF TAXABLE EQUIVALENT YIELDS

MARGINAL TAX BRACKET	TO EQUAL A TAX-FREE YIELD OF:				
	6.0%	7.0%	8.0%	9.0%	10.0%
1987 Brackets:	A TAXABLE BOND WOULD HAVE TO YIELD:				
11%	6.7%	7.9%	9.0%	10.1%	11.2%
15%	7.1	8.2	9.4	10.6	11.8
28%	8.3	9.7	11.1	12.5	13.9
35%	9.2	10.8	12.3	13.8	15.4
38$\frac{1}{2}$%	9.8	11.4	13.0	14.6	16.3
1988 Brackets:					
15%	7.1	8.2	9.4	10.6	11.8
28%	8.3	9.7	11.1	12.5	13.9
33%	9.0	10.4	11.9	13.4	14.9

The table doesn't take state and local income taxes into account. If those taxes are high in your area, a "double tax-free" or "triple tax-free" municipal that avoids those taxes will provide a greater edge than shown in the table. With federal brackets lower, and some state taxes very likely higher, the advantage of double tax-free and triple tax-free municipals over other municipals is likely to increase.

Why are state and local taxes likely to be higher? Many states impose income taxes that are calculated based on federal taxable income. Under the new law, with many deductions reduced or eliminated, taxable income will be higher for many taxpayers. At the federal level, this will be offset by lower tax rates. But if these states do not either lower their rates or change the calculation in other ways, the actual amount of state tax owed may rise considerably.

Miscellaneous Items

For the individual who itemizes deductions, investment expenses (other than investment interest expense) have always been deductible as a miscellaneous deduction. That's still true, but remember that *all* miscellaneous deductions are now subject to the "2% floor" discussed in Chapter 11. And, for the individual investor, the new law takes away an attractive gimmick by ruling out any deduction for travel and meal costs involved in attending investment conventions and seminars (though the registration fee for the convention or seminar remains deductible).

17

THE NEW INVESTMENT BALL GAME

The new tax law will make a profound change in the way people manage their investments. For years, taxable investors have directed much of their efforts toward earning long-term capital gains, which were taxed at significantly lower rates than other types of income. As we saw in Chapter 3, the new tax law makes sharp cuts in the tax rates applied to most types of income; but the preference treatment of long-term capital gains is eliminated—completely eliminated in 1988, with just a drop of preference remaining in 1987 through a special transition rule.

This means that interest, dividends, rents, royalties, and short-term gains are now just as profitable to an investor as long-term gains. Which means, in turn, that investors will have to rethink their strategies, and that in many cases these strategies will be substantially changed.

Managing Your Investments

How should you manage your investments under the new tax law?

It's a new ball game. There is new attraction in all investments that pay taxable interest—bank accounts, bank CDs, money market funds, mortgages (including mortgage-backed securities), and most types of bonds. And there is new attraction in stocks that pay high dividends, such as utilities and oil stocks.

Corporate and Government Bonds

Corporate and government bonds both gain from the drop in tax rates. U.S. Treasury bonds, notes and bills carry the extra advantage of being exempt from state and local taxes, but the yields on Treasuries are often much lower than on comparable corporate bonds (and lower than on municipals, taken on a taxable-equivalent basis). Ginnie Mae securities, which yield more than regular Treasuries, will almost certainly continue to be popular (but note that Ginnie Maes are *not* exempt from state and local taxes).

Tax-Exempt Bonds

As for deciding between taxable and tax-exempt bonds, that's largely a matter of doing the arithmetic to compare your net after-tax yields. Look at the table of taxable equivalent yields in Chapter 16.

The drop in tax rates reduces the attractiveness of tax-exempt bonds, looking strictly at the numbers. But since the new tax law reduces or eliminates many other ways of avoiding taxes, tax-exempt bonds are likely to be in demand as "the only game in town." Also, the new restrictions on tax-exempt bonds mean that fewer such bonds will be issued, reducing the supply. It will take time to see how all these factors combine to affect the prices of tax-exempt bonds, and their attractiveness relative to other investments.

"Total Return"

It's a new ball game—yet it's not as new as it looks. For years, pension managers and managers of other tax-exempt institutional accounts have managed vast sums of money without worrying about the tax distinctions between long-term gains, short-term gains, dividends, and interest. Their approach has helped make popular the concept of "total return," which measures investment performance by combining "appreciation" (or growth in value) with "income," rather than keeping them separate. Now, the individual investor who wants to make money grow over the long term can also take a "total return" approach.

Common Stocks and Your Investment Strategy

It's worth noting that the institutional investment managers have consistently emphasized common stocks as an investment. Why? Some writers think that the end of the tax break on long-term gains makes common stocks less attractive. Relatively speaking, there's some truth in that. But historically, common stocks have been one of the best ways to make your money grow, even without reference to the tax advantage. Over the long term, it seems likely that a well-managed common stock portfolio will continue to outperform bond investments and other fixed income (interest-paying) investments.

"Growth" stocks, if you can identify and select them, will still give you an advantage over most other investments. A stock that grows in value for several years, as you hold it, may not only give you a high "total return" on paper, but will let you avoid tax on the gain until you sell the stock. It's a built-in tax deferral, even if you eventually pay tax on the gain at full rates.

Real Estate

Real estate investments will also continue to be a prime way of making money grow over the long term, often with the same type of tax deferral. But, as with common stocks, the emphasis will have to be on research and selection rather than on tax advantages.

Research

In all investment areas, the new ball game will involve careful research and attention to the basic economics of an investment. Is this new? Hardly—or, if it is, it shows the extent to which investment priorities have been distorted by tax considerations.

As always, investment rewards will be best for those who are not part of the crowd. As people adjust to the new tax bill, thinking for yourself will be critically important. Remember that the markets already reflect many of the factors described above. If popularity drives up the prices of investments obviously favored by the new law, don't hesitate to look for good values in neglected areas, whether they be growth investments, tax-exempt bonds, or any others. (But remember that if you *borrow* to invest, the interest you pay won't be deductible unless you have taxable investment income to cover it.)

Mutual Funds

Investors concerned about the problem of selecting individual investments should consider the possibilities of mutual funds. In recent years there has been a proliferation of funds for every objective—common stock funds, bond funds, tax-exempt bond funds, specialized stock funds, money market funds, etc. While the profusion of funds can be confusing, fund performance, yields, and other facts and statistics are tracked and reported regularly by *Money* magazine, *Barron's*, *Forbes*, *Changing Times*, and other popular periodicals.

18

TAX SHELTERS

In an unexpectedly broad move, the Tax Reform Act of 1986 completely sweeps away most "tax shelter" arrangements.

What Is a Tax Shelter?

A tax shelter, in general parlance, is an investment creating artificial paper losses that can be taken as tax deductions against other types of income, such as salaries, regular business income, interest, dividends, etc. Many high-bracket taxpayers have used tax shelters to reduce or eliminate income taxes on basically large incomes. Many taxpayers in more modest brackets have used small real estate investments, or tax shelter packages marketed by brokerage firms, for the same purpose.

Passive Activities

The new law wipes out most of these arrangements by creating a new category of "passive activities." Losses in these activities ("passive losses") can only be deducted against income from the same type of activity ("passive income"). Passive losses can't be deducted against earned income, ordinary investment income, or income from an active business or profession.

A "passive activity" is roughly defined as an activity where the taxpayer has an ownership interest but does not "materially participate" in the business. Often such interests are in the form of limited partnerships. Also, by definition, rental of real estate or other real property is considered a passive activity under the new law, with an important exception to be noted below.

For passive-type activities entered into after January 1, 1987, the new rules apply in full immediately. For such activities entered into earlier, the deductibility of losses against other types of income will be phased out on the same 5-year schedule as the consumer interest deduction:

Year	Percent of Loss Deductible
1986	100%
1987	65%
1988	40%
1989	20%
1990	10%
1991 and after	0%

Exceptions to the New Rules

There are a few exceptions to the new rules—not many. For many people, the most important exception is one applying to rental real estate, which will be described in Chapter 19. Working interests in oil and gas properties are exempted from the rule, but only if the form of ownership does not limit the taxpayer's liability, which rules out limited partnership arrangements. And there are a few more specialized exceptions.

The new rules are expected to be broadly effective. There will still be ways of investing to generate income that is effectively tax-free. But the creation of artificial losses to offset noninvestment income should be cut to a trickle.

Investment in passive activities will not end, but there will be more stress on passive investments that produce income rather than losses—such as income-producing real estate or oil and gas properties. An investor who has passive losses that are no longer usable can replace some ordinary investments with investments that produce passive income. The passive income can then be offset by the passive losses, and the investor will in effect have found a way of making a certain amount of investment income tax-free.

Also, although passive losses are disallowed, they

may be carried forward for use against passive income in future years. If such use is not available, they will reduce the gain or increase the loss when the passive investment is eventually sold.

Who Needs Shelter?

So attempts to shelter income from taxes will certainly continue. But with tax rates dramatically reduced at higher income levels, perhaps the big news about shelters is that even where they still exist, they have become far less important. The tax bite isn't what it used to be. If an executive earns a $300,000 salary, and then gets a $100,000 bonus, and only has to pay $28,000 of that bonus in tax to the federal government, rather than $50,000 as previously—who needs a tax shelter?

19

REAL ESTATE

The real estate industry has won many political battles over the years. In the Tax Reform Act of 1986, the results were mixed. After a rousing battle, the critical tax advantages enjoyed by homeowners were largely continued. But people who invest in real estate as a business, either as a full-time activity or as a sideline, have had their previous advantages sharply curtailed.

Your Residence

If you own a home (or two homes), the new law continues to let you deduct mortgage interest on your primary and second residences. (See Chapter 9.) And state and local property taxes remain deductible. (See Chapter 8.)

Sale of Your Home

The new law preserves the special tax breaks on sale of your *principal residence*. Generally, if you sell your principal residence, and you buy a new home within two years before or after the sale that costs as much as the selling price of the old home, any capital gains tax on the sale is deferred until you sell the new home (when the process can be repeated). If the new home costs less than the selling price of the old, only the part of the gain that has been reinvested can be deferred.

One-Time Exclusion

If you are *age 55 or over*, and you sell your principal residence in which you have lived for at least 3 out of the last

5 years, there is a once-per-lifetime exclusion by which $125,000 of the gain on the sale can be completely excluded from your income and remain permanently free from tax.

Reporting Real Estate Transactions

Under the new legislation, all real estate transactions must be reported by whoever is responsible for closing the sale. This provision is effective for all sales of property beginning January 1, 1987.

Real Estate Investments

If you invest in real estate, apart from your own home (or two homes), the new law greatly reduces your tax advantages. As we saw in Chapter 18, real estate investments, and any investments where you lease out real estate or other real property, are now considered "passive activities," and any expenses incurred in these activities (passive expenses) can only be deducted against income from the same type of activity (passive income). With a few exceptions, losses from real estate can no longer be deducted against earned income or regular investment income.

An Important Exception

One of the exceptions is especially important to a wide range of smaller real estate investors. Losses of up to $25,000 from real estate rental activities can be deducted from other types of income (nonpassive income) if you meet three tests:

1. You must own at least 10% of the property.
2. You must "actively participate" in management of the property.
3. Your adjusted gross income (AGI) must not exceed $100,000 in order to take the full $25,000 deduction against ordinary income. If your AGI is between $100,000 and $150,000, the deduction is phased out;

above $150,000, it disappears, and rental losses can only be deducted against other passive income.

The Tax Reform Act will cut into the attractiveness of many real estate investments. Remember, however, that the new rule preventing you from deducting passive losses against ordinary income is being phased in over 5 years. (The table in Chapter 18 shows how the percent of losses deductible is reduced year-by-year.)

Tax Credits

There are a few other exceptions for real estate in the new tax law. Tax *credits* (not deductions) for those who rehabilitate certain older buildings have been curtailed but not eliminated. If you rehabilitate a nonresidential building that dates originally from before 1936, you are entitled to a tax credit of up to 10% of the cost (previously 15% or 20%, with looser age limits). If you rehabilitate a certified historic structure, the tax credit is up to 20% (previously 25%). There are also special new credits available to those who buy, build or rehabilitate low-income housing. For any taxpayer, all these credits together can be used to offset the tax on up to $25,000 of nonpassive income; but the use of the credits is phased out for taxpayers with an adjusted gross income of between $200,000 and $250,000.

Depreciation

The new law changes the depreciation schedules on all types of assets. Under the old law, real estate investors could take depreciation write-offs at relatively rapid rates, reducing taxable income in the early years and often creating paper losses (which were deductible against ordinary income). The new law is much less favorable. For residential properties put in service beginning in 1987, depreciation will be on a straight-line basis over 27.5 years; for other real estate, it will be on a straight-line basis over 31.5 years.

Capital Gains

One of the advantages of real estate investment under the old tax law was the reduced tax on long-term capital gains, which applied when a property was eventually sold. Under the new law, as we have seen, this tax break is gone—offset in part by the general reduction in rates.

PART V
MISCELLANEOUS
PROVISIONS

20

IF YOU OWN YOUR OWN BUSINESS

The Tax Reform Act of 1986 makes far-reaching changes in the ways businesses are taxed. Most of these changes are outside the scope of this book. However, we will summarize a few of the most significant changes, especially those of importance to the self-employed businessperson or professional, or the person who has part-time self-employed income.

Repeal of Investment Tax Credit

The investment tax credit, amounting to 6% or 10% of the cost of equipment, is repealed for property put in service after December 31, 1985. Transition rules apply to equipment previously contracted for, and carryforward credits will be reduced by up to 35%. While the repeal has been publicized for its sharp effects on heavy industry, it also will affect many small businesses and certain professionals.

Depreciation

The new law makes wide changes in depreciation schedules. Write-offs will be faster in some cases, slower in others. For real estate, write-offs will be much slower and less favorable (see Chapter 19). For smaller businesses, the amount of investment that can be deducted immediately as an expense is raised from $5,000 to $10,000.

Accounting Methods

The Act changes the accounting rules that apply to many businesses. Obviously, businesspersons and professionals will need to consult with their accountants regarding application of all the new provisions of the Act.

Business or Hobby?

If a taxpayer engages in an activity for profit, it is a trade or business. In this case, all expenses are generally deductible, and any loss can be deducted against other income. But if the activity is a hobby, expenses can be deducted only to the extent of income from the hobby; and the expenses must be taken as itemized deductions, subject to the 2% floor.

Several factors affect the determination as to whether an activity is a business or a hobby. Under the old law, an activity could be presumed to be for profit if it showed a profit for two or more out of five consecutive years. Under the new law, the presumption holds only if the activity shows a profit in *three* or more out of five consecutive years.

There's still an exception for horse breeding, training, showing, or racing. As before, these activities need only show a profit in two out of seven years.

Business Use of Home

As we noted in Chapter 11, the IRS has always been sensitive regarding deductions for the business use of a home, whether by employees or self-employed persons. If you take deductions for the use of your home in a trade, business or profession, the new law tightens the rules to prevent the home office deduction from creating a loss that could be deducted against other income. In general terms, home office deductions will be allowed only to the extent that the activity shows a profit before taking these deductions into account. (However, expenses not deducted may be carried forward.)

Business Meals and Entertainment

Beginning in 1987, under the new law, only 80% of the cost of business meals and business entertainment will be deductible. There are exceptions, but they are generally minor. Moreover, the rules are tightened in an attempt to ensure that meals are deducted only if they have a direct business purpose.

Additional restrictions are placed on the cost of sports tickets as a business expense. Generally, only the face value of the tickets will be deductible. Also, the extra cost of luxury "skybox" tickets over the cost of regular box seats will be phased out as a deduction over three years. (After these limitations, the deductions for the cost of tickets will still be subject to the general 80% rule stated above.)

Business Travel

The new law puts a limit (in terms of cost per day) on the deduction for business-related travel by cruise or other luxury ships. However, if the expense is for a convention that takes place on the cruise ship, it remains fully deductible.

Travel expenses that used to be deductible because of the educational value of the travel will no longer be deductible. Nor will travel expenses incurred to attend a meeting or convention on investments.

Self-Employed Health Insurance

For the first time, a self-employed person will be able to deduct 25% of the premiums paid for health insurance, on the condition that the insurance be available to all employees on a nondiscriminatory basis. The new law extends this provision only through 1989.

Performing Artists

Performing artists below a certain income level may be able to deduct expenses on the more favorable basis allowed to independent contractors rather than as employees. See Chapter 11.

Corporate Tax Rates

The new tax law broadly lowers the corporate income tax rates. Here's how the new schedule compares with the old:

CORPORATE TAX RATES

Old Law		New Law	
Taxable Income	Rate	Taxable Income	Rate
$0-$25,000	15%	$0-$50,000	15%
25,000-50,000	18%	50,000-75,000	25%
50,000-75,000	30%	Over $75,000	34%(b)
75,000-100,000	40%		
Over $100,000	46%(a)		

(a) Additional 5% surtax on income from $1,000,000 to $1,405,000 (maximum surtax $20,250)
(b) Additional 5% surtax on income from $100,000 to $335,000 (maximum surtax $11,750).

Since the new rates don't apply until July 1, 1987, the actual rates for calendar year 1987 are a blend of the old and the new.

For corporations, under the old law, the maximum tax on capital gains was 28%. The new law abolishes the special treatment of capital gains, so that the maximum rate will be 34%.

Note that the highest corporate tax rate (34%) is now higher than the highest individual tax rate (28%), and that the various surtaxes don't basically change the comparison. This may affect the forms of organization chosen by businesses, and may be an incentive to elect "S corporation" status, under which corporate earnings are attributed directly to the shareholders for tax purposes.

Alternative Minimum Tax on Corporations

The new law creates an alternative minimum tax (AMT) on corporations in order to tax earnings that are not subject, or only lightly subject, to the regular corporate income tax. Application of the new tax is complicated, but basically the law gives each corporation a $40,000 exemption and puts a flat tax of 20% on all income above that level. If this calculation produces a higher tax than under the regular tax schedules, the corporation must pay the higher figure.

Dividends Received Deduction

The old law permitted a corporation to deduct 85% of the dividends it received from other domestic corporations, and only be taxed on 15%. The new law reduces the deduction to 80%, making the taxable portion 20%. Various exceptions still apply.

21

ALTERNATIVE MINIMUM TAX

The alternative minimum tax (AMT) is an alternative method of tax computation intended to impose a meaningful tax on individuals who have substantial income but who otherwise would pay little or no tax because of "tax preference" items on their tax returns.

The AMT must be paid if its computation results in a higher tax liability than using the regular tax computation.

Computing the Alternative Minimum Tax

Computation of the AMT begins with a taxpayer's regular adjusted gross income. The taxpayer then subtracts the following exemptions, depending on filing status:

Status	Exemption
Married filing jointly	$40,000
Single or Head of Household	30,000
Married filing separately	20,000

Under the new law, the above exemptions will be phased out at higher income levels, being reduced by 25% of the amount by which "alternative minimum taxable income" exceeds $150,000 for married couples filing jointly, $112,500 for single filers, and $75,000 for marrieds filing separately.

Preference Items

To find "alternative minimum taxable income," the taxpayer adds back certain specified "tax preference" items that either were nontaxable income or created special deductions when tax liability was computed in the regular manner. The definition of preference items is technical and requires the assistance of a lawyer or accountant, but the list includes certain types of depreciation and depletion allowances, many tax shelter deductions, the 60% exclusion applied to long-term capital gains (through 1986 only), certain benefits involved in incentive stock options, and others. Beginning in 1987, the list will also include any passive losses that were deducted in the regular tax calculation, the appreciation in property contributed to charities, and the interest received on certain tax-exempt bonds issued after August 7, 1986 that are classified as "private-purpose" bonds (see Chapter 16).

21% Tax Rate

After all the preferences are added back to arrive at "alternative minimum taxable income," the alternative minimum tax rate is applied. Previously the AMT rate was 20%; the new law raises it to 21%, beginning in 1987. The taxpayer must then pay the higher of (1) his/her regular tax liability calculated without the AMT, or (2) his/her tax liability under the AMT.

22

TAXES AND CHILDREN

Taxation of Grantor Trusts

A grantor trust is a trust established by a donor who retains benefits or control over it. The *undistributed* income of new and existing grantor trusts will be taxed under the new law according to the following rates:

Undistributed Income	Tax Rate
$0–$5,000	15%
5,000 or more	28%

For trust income between $13,000 and $25,000, the benefits of the 15% bracket will be phased out by a surtax, similar to the surtax applied on individual returns.

Distributed income of grantor trusts will be taxed at the child's rate—which, as explained below, will in effect be the parents' rate for children under age 14.

The new law specifically states that trusts must use the calendar year for reporting. All tax rate changes affecting trusts are effective beginning March 15, 1987. For the calendar year 1987, accordingly, trusts will be taxed at a blended tax rate.

Clifford Trusts and Spousal Remainder Trusts

Clifford and Spousal Remainder trusts—classic methods of shifting taxable income to children and other dependents or relatives taxed at lower tax rates—have been specifically eliminated by the new Act. The rules regarding these trusts are effective retroactively, beginning on March 1, 1986. However, trusts created before that date are still effective.

A Clifford Trust is one where the assets remain in trust for the benefit of a named beneficiary for a minimum period of 10 years and one day. After that time, or longer, the assets revert back to the grantor, the person who originally gave them. In a Spousal Remainder

Trust, one spouse puts assets in trust for the benefit of a named beneficiary. There is no minimum required time period; when the trust terminates, the assets become the property of the grantor's spouse.

Unearned Income of Child Under Age 14

In general, all unearned income of a child under age 14 in excess of $500, from whatever source, will be taxed under the new law as if it had been added to the parents' income, if the parents' tax rate is higher than the child's. This applies to income from savings accounts, trusts, custodial accounts under the Uniform Gifts to Minors Act, etc., etc.

Since the child may take a standard deduction of $500 against unearned income, the tax on the unearned income of a child under 14 will work as follows:

Unearned Income	Tax Rate
0–$ 500	**None** (standard or itemized deduction)
500–1,000	**Child's** rates
Over 1,000	**Higher** of parents' or child's rates

Financing Education

Traditional income-shifting techniques, a major way to build up money to finance education, have been swept away by the new law which specifically disallows Clifford Trusts and Spousal Remainder Trusts and eliminates the tax advantage of other methods. However, remember that the unearned income of a child age 14 or older is not taxed at the parents' rate. Parents may want to think of investing for children in assets such as Series EE U.S. Savings Bonds, on which earnings can be deferred for tax purposes until the child reaches age 14.

Remember also that the drop in tax rates under the new law reduces the tax bite on all investment income, other than capital gains, and means that money can be accumulated for the future with less need to look for specific tax breaks. (See the discussion of investment strategy in Chapter 17.)

Generation-Skipping Tax

The new law tightens the application of the generation-skipping tax—an additional tax paid when individuals receive gifts or bequests from persons who are more than one generation older than the recipient. In practice, this tax applies only to extremely wealthy people and to very large gifts or bequests.

Until 1990, a person may give up to $2,000,000 to each grandchild without incurring the generation-skipping tax. In addition, up to a total of $1,000,000 in generation-skipping transfers to nongrandchildren may be made. After 1990, the $2,000,000-per-grandchild exemption is eliminated.

Adoption Expenses

Beginning in 1987, the itemized deduction of up to $1,500 for the costs of adopting a child with special needs is eliminated. However, the Adoption Assistance program in the Social Security Act is amended to provide financial aid in such situations.

Child and Dependent Care Credit

The new law maintains the existing child and dependent care credit. See Chapter 11.

Social Security Numbers for Children

On tax returns filed after 1987, the new law requires all children or other dependents age 5 years or older to be identified by Social Security numbers if they are claimed as dependents. This is to prevent both parents from claiming an exemption for the same child on their tax returns if they are divorced or file separate returns.

To obtain a Social Security number for a child, file Form SS-5, obtainable at your local Social Security Administration office.

23

SCHOLARSHIPS AND GRANTS

Under the prior act, scholarships, grants and certain awards were generally not taxed. Under the new law, certain of these categories are now taxable.

Scholarships and Grants

The new Act limits the benefits of the exclusion to degree candidates. Moreover, it taxes scholarships, fellowships, and grants of degree candidates to the extent of any amounts in excess of the amounts spent on tuition and course-related books and equipment. This means that any scholarship or grant money used by a student to pay for room, board, and noncourse-related expenses will be taxed as income to the student. These changes are effective beginning in 1987, but do not apply to any scholarships or fellowships granted before August 17, 1986, which continue to be treated as under the old law.

Prizes and Awards

Prizes and awards are generally taxable. However, the old law made an exception for awards for scientific, artistic, charitable or similar achievement, such as the Nobel Prizes. The new law eliminates this exception unless the recipient donates the prize money to charity.

24

INCOME AVERAGING AND OTHER MISCELLANY

Income Averaging

Under certain circumstances, the prior law allowed a taxpayer to choose income averaging, which in effect allowed part of any large "bulge" in income to be taxed as if spread over 4 years. The new tax act eliminates income averaging. However, note that the need for income averaging is reduced by the drop in tax rates.

Withholding

The tax withholding tables will be revised to reflect the new tax rates. All employees must must file a revised form W-4 with their employer before October 1, 1987; otherwise the employer must withhold taxes as if the employee claimed only one exemption if single, or two if married.

Estimated Taxes

The new law revises the requirements for paying estimated taxes. Beginning in 1987, to avoid a penalty, your estimated payments must equal the lesser of (a) 100% of your actual tax for the prior year or (b) 90% (rather than 80% as formerly) of the current tax liability.

Penalties

The penalty for a "substantial" understatement of tax liability has been increased from 10% to 20% of the underpayment, beginning with tax returns due after 1986.

Miscellaneous Reporting Requirements

Beginning with tax returns for 1987, amounts and sources of tax-exempt interest received must be listed on your tax return. The interest remains nontaxable, but must be reported.

TABLES
HOW THE TAX RATES CHANGE 1986–1988

The following tables show the effects of the decline in the basic tax rates and the increases in the standard deduction and personal exemption. They do not show the effects of the new law on the many changes in allowable deductions or the effect on larger families.

TABLE A

MARRIED TAXPAYERS FILING JOINTLY*

WAGES	TAX		
	1986	1987	1988
$ 10,000	$ 480	$ 270	$ 170
20,000	1,980	1,740	1,670
35,000	5,330	3,990	3,920
50,000	10,020	8,120	7,650
75,000	19,770	16,690	14,640
100,000	30,430	25,530	22,600
150,000	54,120	44,780	39,100
225,000	91,350	73,650	61,600

*All amounts rounded to nearest $10. Table assumes standard deduction, no dependents, and wages as the sole source of income.

Source: Price Waterhouse

TABLE B

SINGLE TAXPAYERS*

WAGES	TAX		
	1986	1987	1988
$ 10,000	$ 860	$ 760	$ 760
20,000	2,790	2,260	2,260
35,000	7,120	6,560	6,100
50,000	12,870	11,800	10,400
75,000	24,230	21,130	18,640
100,000	36,440	30,760	26,890
150,000	61,440	50,010	41,160
225,000	98,940	78,880	62,160

*All amounts rounded to nearest $10. Table assumes standard deduction, no dependents, and wages as the sole source of income.

Source: Price Waterhouse

TABLE C

HEAD OF HOUSEHOLD*

WAGES	TAX		
	1986	1987	1988
$ 10,000	$ 790	$ 740	$ 550
20,000	2,590	2,240	2,050
35,000	6,620	5,470	4,920
50,000	11,830	10,200	9,120
75,000	22,590	18,950	16,470
100,000	34,160	28,240	24,720
150,000	58,790	47,490	40,770
225,000	96,300	76,370	61,770

*All amounts rounded to nearest $10. Table assumes standard deduction, no dependents, and wages as the sole source of income.

Source: Price Waterhouse

BIOGRAPHY—PHYLLIS C. KAUFMAN

Phyllis C. Kaufman, the originator of the *No-Nonsense Guides*, is a Philadelphia attorney and theatrical producer. A graduate of Brandeis University, she was an editor of the law review at Temple University School of Law. She is listed in *Who's Who in American Law*, *Who's Who in American Women* and *Foremost Women of the Twentieth Century*.

BIOGRAPHY—ARNOLD CORRIGAN

Arnold Corrigan, noted financial expert, is the author of *How Your IRA Can Make You a Millionaire* and a frequent guest on financial talk shows. A senior officer of a large New York investment advisory firm, he holds Bachelor's and Master's Degrees in economics from Harvard and has written for *Barron's* and other financial publications.